D1173731

MASAHISA FUKASE
FAMILY

7

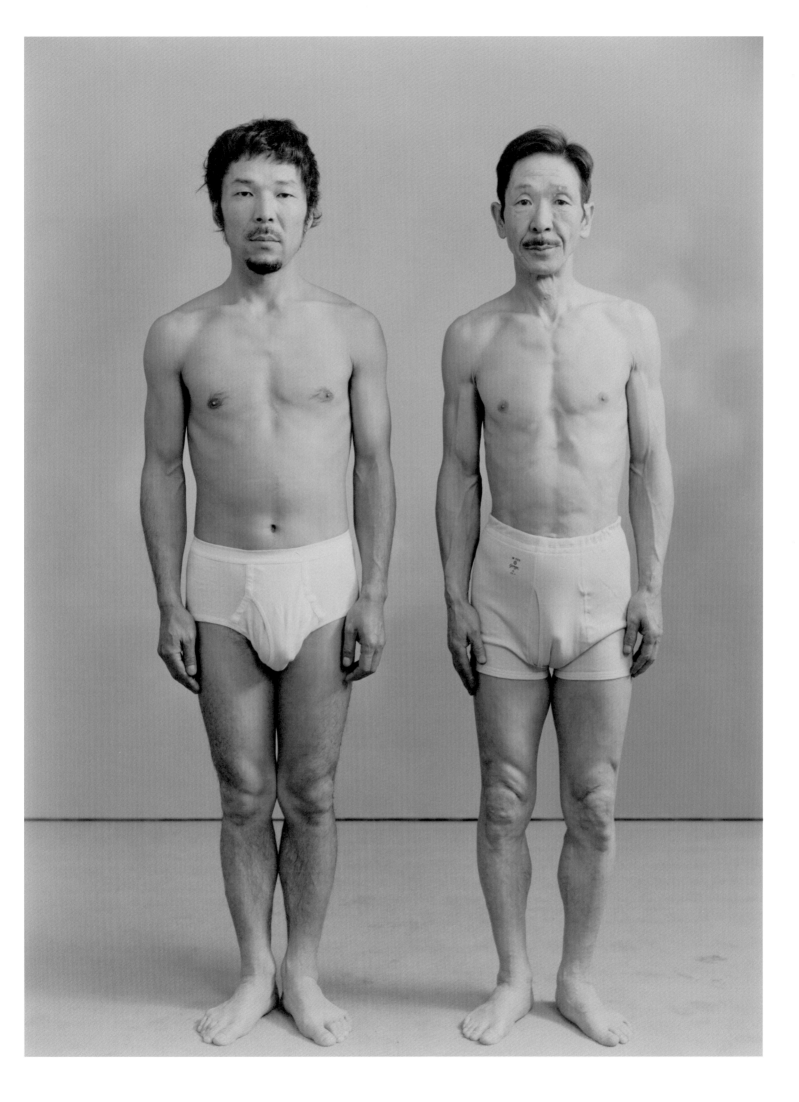

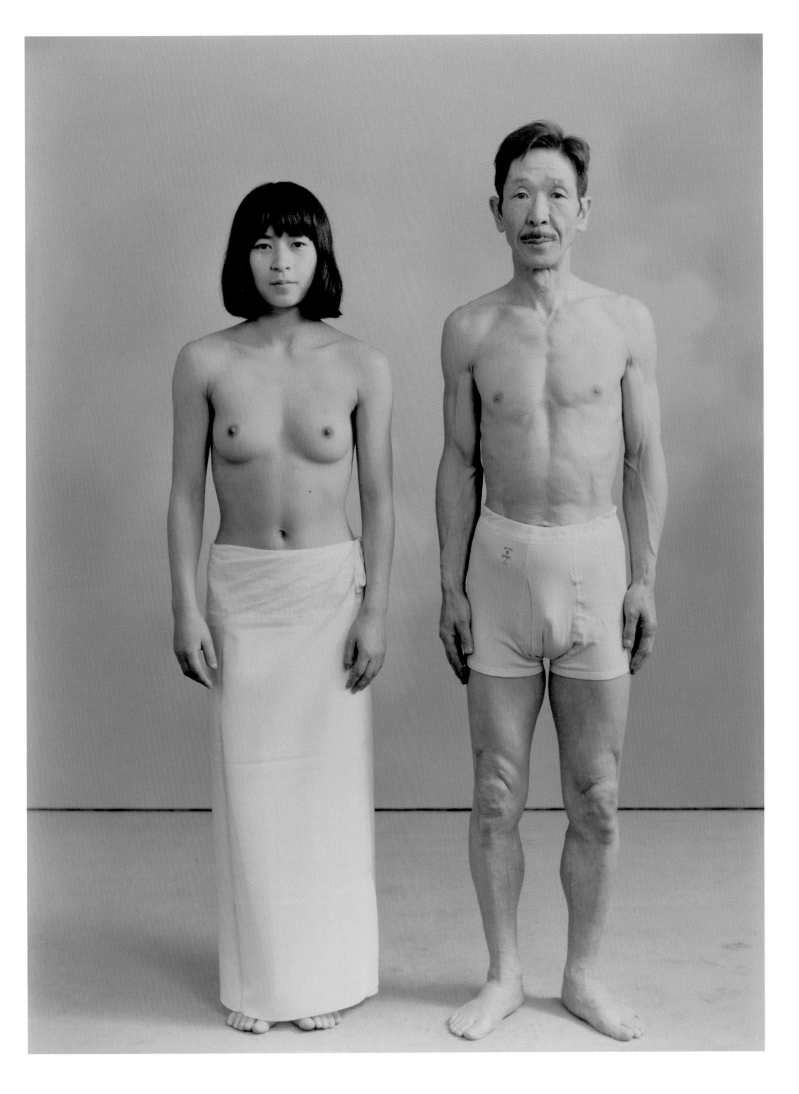

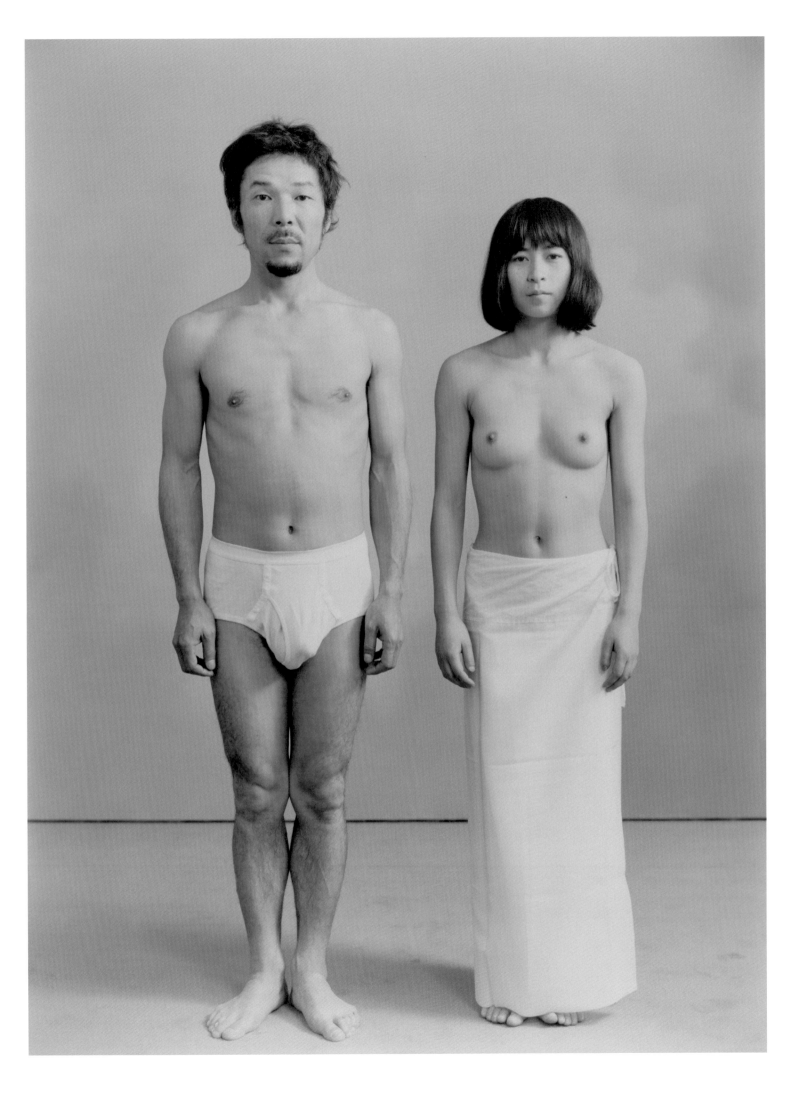

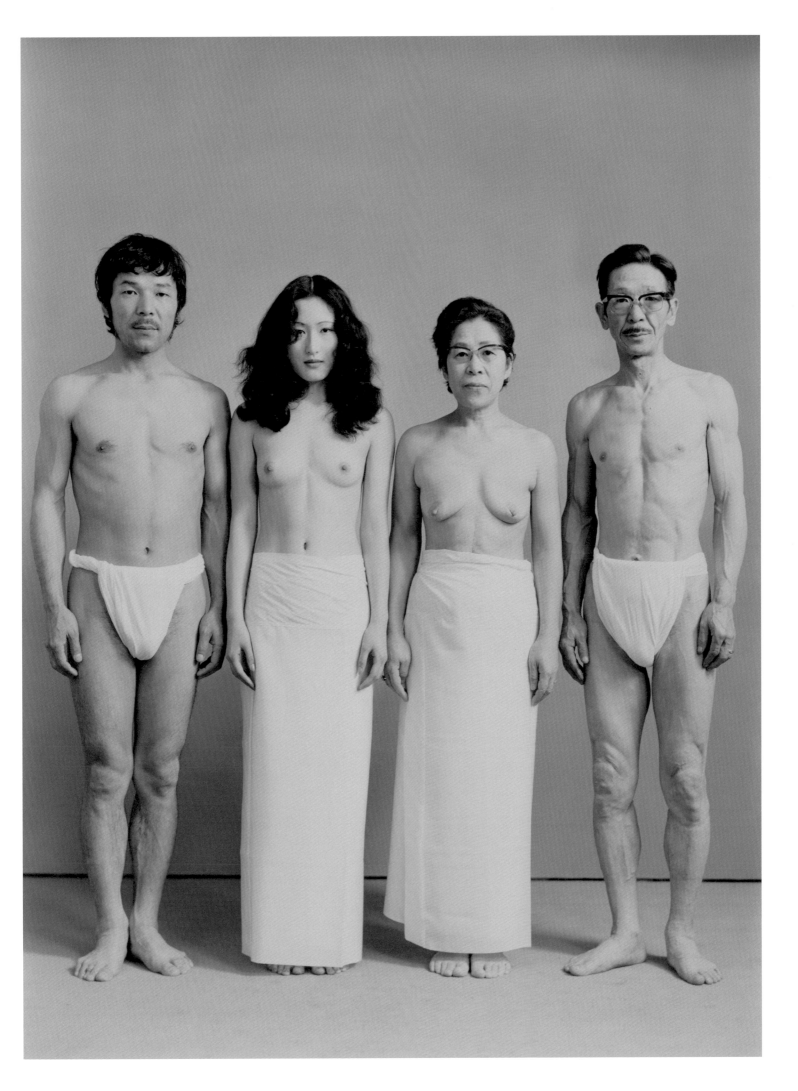

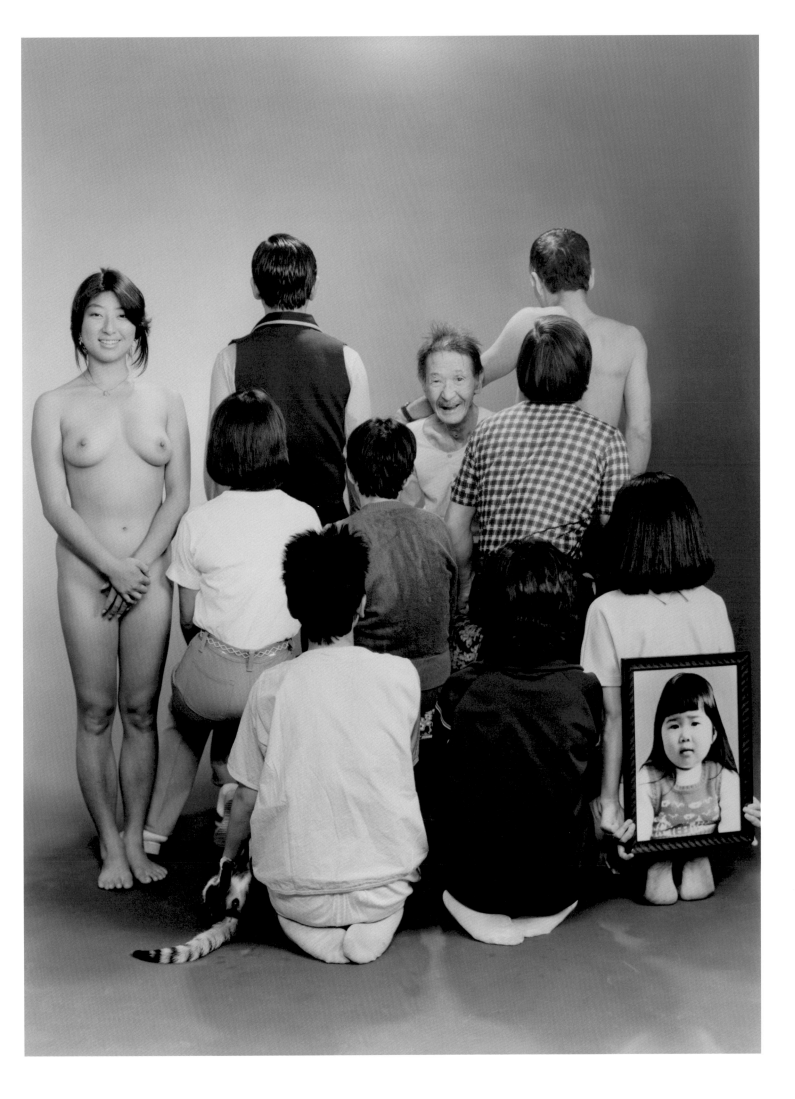

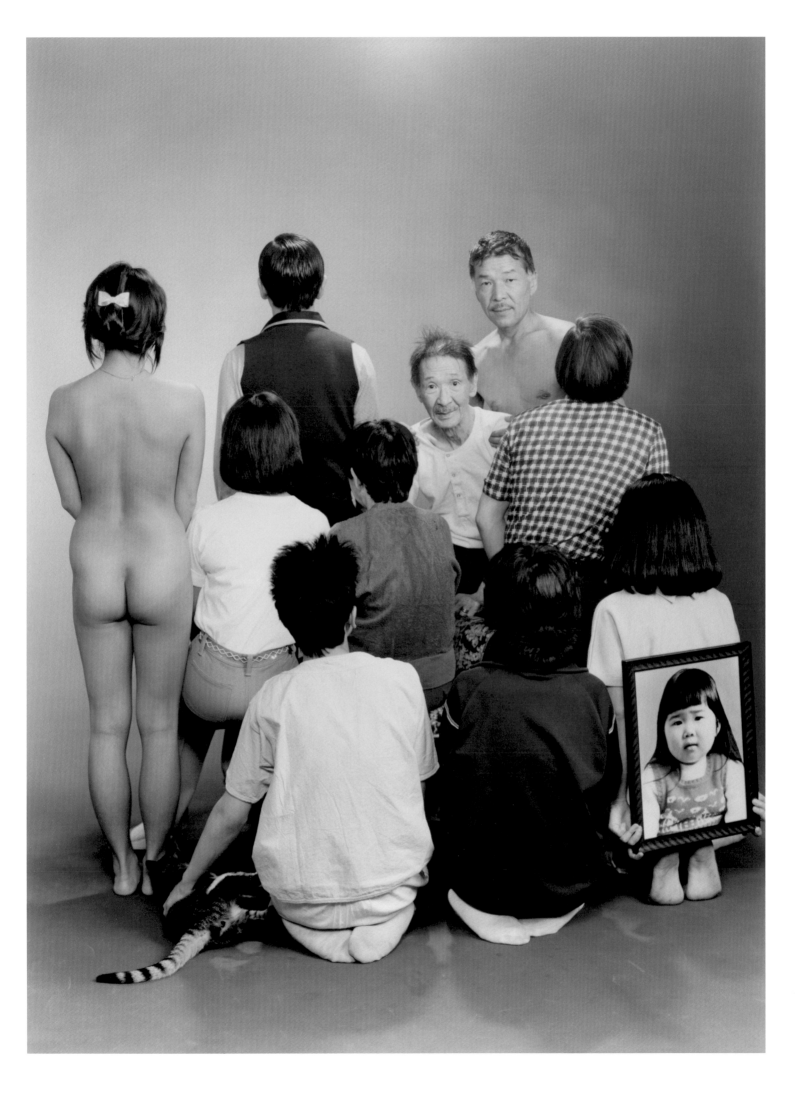

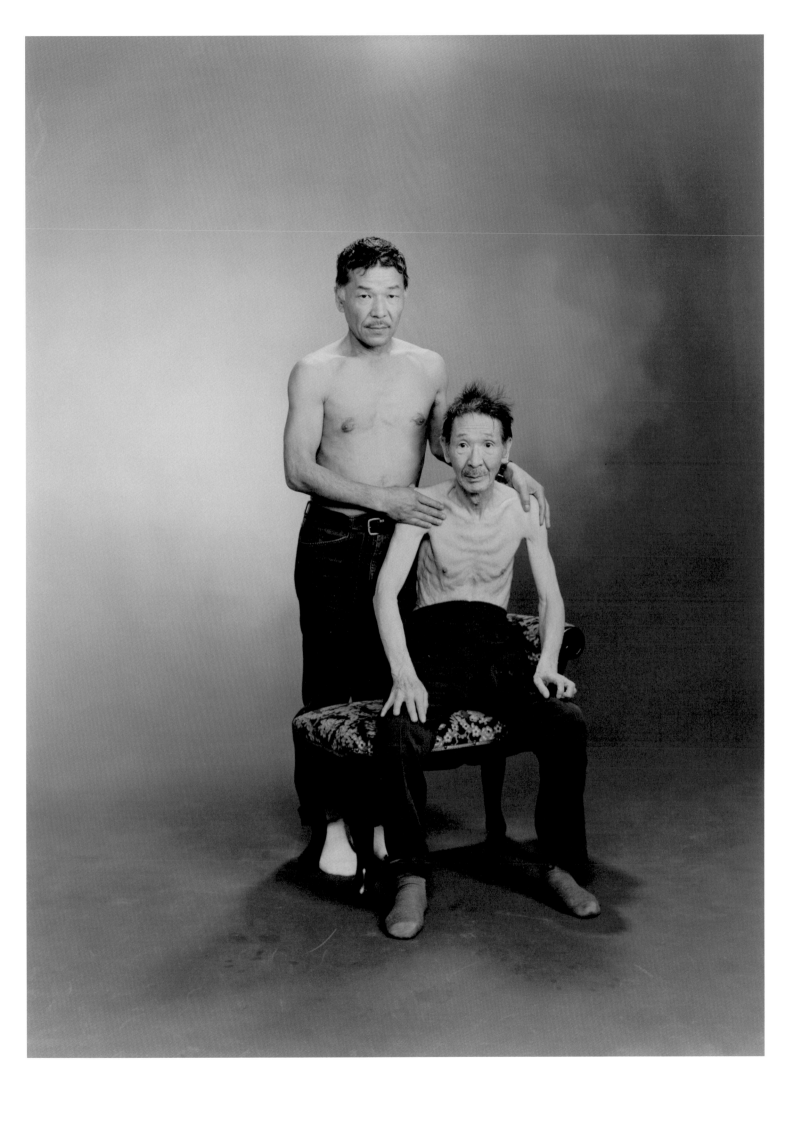

1. 1974 The Fukase Photo Studio

2. 1971 Upper row, left to right: My wife, Yoko; my younger brother, Toshiteru; my father, Sukezo; Hisashi Daikoji, my sister's husband. Lower row, left to right: Akiko, Toshiteru's wife; Gaku, my sister's son; my mother Mitsue; Kyoko, Toshiteru's daughter; my sister Kanako and Takuya, Toshiteru's son.

3. 1971 Variation on Photograph 2.

4. 1971 Variation on Photographs 2, and 3.

5. 1971 Variation on Photographs 2, 3, and 4.

6. 1972 On the left is H, a dancer. Others as in Photograph 2.

7. 1972 On the left is M, a singer. Others as in Photograph 2.

8. 1972 On the left is K, an actor. Others as in Photograph 2.

9. 1972 Variation on Photograph 8.

10. 1972 Sukezo and Mitsue.

11. 1972 Masahisa and Sukezo.

12. 1972 K, an actor, and Sukezo.

13. 1972 Masahisa and K, an actor.

14. 1972 Variation on Photograph 13.

15. 1972 On the left is O, an apprentice actor. Others as in Photograph 2, but with the addition of Miyako, my sister's daughter.

16. 1972 Variation on Photograph 15.

17. 1972 Masahisa, apprentice actor O, Mitsue, and Sukezo.

18. 1974 Sukezo.

19. 1974 Mitsue.

20. 1974 Masahisa.

21. 1974 Upper row, from left to right: Masahisa, Toshiteru, Sukezo, Hisashi Daikoji. Bottom row, from left to right: Akiko and Gaku, Mitsue and Kyoko, Kanako and Miyako, Takuya.

22. 1974 Masahisa.

23. 1974 Masahisa and Yoko.

24. 1975 Upper row, from left to right: Masahisa, Toshiteru, Sukezo, Hisashi Daikoji. Bottom row, from left to right: Akiko and Gaku, Mitsue and Kyoko, Kanako and Miyako, Takuya.

25. 1975 Variation on Photograph 24.

26. 1985 Upper row, from left to right: A, a model; Toshiteru, Sukezo, Masahisa. Middle row: Akiko, Mitsue, Hisashi Daikoji. Bottom row, from left to right: Gaku, Kyoko, Kanako, and a memorial portrait of Miyako, 1985.

27. 1985 Variation on Photograph 26.

28. 1985 Variation on Photograph 26 and 27.

29. 1985 Masahisa and Sukezo.

30. 1985 Upper row, from left to right: Masahisa, Toshiteru, Mitsue. Middle row, left to right: Akiko, Sukezo, Hisashi Daikoji. Bottom row, from left to right: Kyoko, Kanako, and a memorial portrait of Miyako.

31. 1985 Variation on Photograph 30.

32. 1987 Upper row, from left to right: Masahisa, Toshiteru, a memorial portrait of Sukezo, Takuya. Middle row, from left to right: Akiko, Mitsue and Hisashi Daikoji. Bottom row, from left to right: Gaku, Kyoko, Kanako, and a memorial portrait of Miyako.

33. 1989 From left to right: Masahisa, Toshiteru, and a memorial portrait of Sukezo and Mitsue.

34. 1990 The Fukase Photo Studio after the family business closed.

深瀬昌久, 1991

記憶の中の私は、いつも人にかこまれていた。血縁の人達、近所の友達、生家の前にあった三本のアカシヤや、国民学校の入り口のニレの巨木までが、今の私には懐かしいというか、なにか人格化されて感じられる。私は今57歳だから、やはり人並みに老境に入った証というべきかもしれない。

「ゆく河の流れは絶えずして、しかも、もとの水にあらず。淀みに浮ぶうたかたは、かつ消えかつ結びて、久しくとどまりたるためしなし。世中にある人と栖と、またかくのごとし......」(方丈記)

父は4年前に亡くなり、母も一昨年特別養護老人ホームに入った。弟は離婚し、その息子と娘は母と東京で自活している。妹夫婦は国鉄民営化で退職し、札幌郊外のスーパーのマネージャーになった。私の生家の「深瀬写真館」は人手に渡り、家族は四散した。

私は、北海道の北端部に位置する中川郡美深町東一条北2丁目21番地で生まれた。父は助造、母はみつゑ、祖父の庸光は山形県からの屯田兵として入植し、日露戦争には陸軍伍長として従軍した。祖母みやのは同じ山形県庄内の足軽の娘だったという。祖父がどこで写真術を修得したかはわからないが、明治41年上川支庁写真師鑑札をとって美深町に半農半写(?)の写真館を開業、母はその次女として明治45年に生まれている。父助造は大正元年、美深町に近い風連村の農家の三男に生まれ、尋常小学校高等科を出るとすぐ村の写真館に丁稚奉公に出され2年ほどたって札幌の茶屋商店に移るが、すぐ「出写し」、つまり半月から一月単位で町や村の祭りや式事を巡り、注文写真を写したという。

これは、私も中学生のころ、父の命令でやらされたものだ。お正月三が日は音威子府駅前の旅館の入り口に「深瀬写真館出張所」の幟を立てて客を待ち、近郷の村祭りには綿あめ屋と並んで写真見本を並べたが、正直いってとても恥ずかしく嫌だった。

どのようなわけで父母が見合いをして養子縁組をするにいたったかはもう知る人はいないが、昭和8年5月吉日に結婚式をあげ、その記念写真は祖父が写したのであろう。

写真屋にあきあきしていた祖父はただちに隠居の身となって父が二代目を継ぎ、昭和9年に私が生まれる。子供のころの父は、とても怖かった。短気で癇性でちょっとしたことで怒鳴りまくったので、私は温和しく利口な子供だったが、父の前ではいつもびくびくしていたように思う。

写真館は繁盛して、お正月とかお祭り、卒業式とか入学式などの祝日は、家の前に写真を写していただくための、長い行列ができた。当時、写真館は町のエリートだった。

父は、撮影と乾板の現像（まだフイルムではなくガラス乾板）、そして鼻筋をたてたり口許を引締めたり肩を濃くしたりする修正技術なら自分より上手はいない、と自慢だった。母は焼きつけの担当だった。炭ストーブを焚いた酢の臭いのつんと鼻をつく小さな暗室に、私の目の高さほどの密着焼付機があって、乾板の濃さによってイチ・ニイー・サン・シーとつぶやきながら露光する母のそばにいた私は、たぶん3歳か4歳だっただろう。母は一酸化炭素中毒で暗室でよく倒れたものだった。6歳のころには、私も水洗を手伝わされた。手押ポンプで大きなバットにぎっしり入った合版（手札）や中版（キャビネ）の写真をかきまぜては水を汲み、水を切ってはまたポンプを押す。真冬などは冷たさに手の感覚がなくなった。

小学校1年生のときに大東亜戦争が始まって、尋常小学校は国民学校に変わっていた。2年生のとき、弟の了暉が生まれた。大本営発表はいつも「勝った勝った」のお祭りさわぎで、「鬼畜米英、撃ちてし止まぬ」と標語だけは勇ましかったが、食糧を始め物資は確実に窮乏していって、「欲しがりません勝つまでは」とやせ我慢していた。

父が丙種合格で旭川歩兵師団に入営した。学校はいつしか援農という名の農家の手伝い集団となり、脚にゲートルを巻いては畑の草むしりをさせられた。写真材料なども全く手に入らず、町の商店全部が開店休業になった。年寄り子供を除いて、男は招集された。お寺の鐘や火鉢や火箸とかの金物類はもちろん、私の可愛がっていた猫のタマまで寒地の兵隊さんの襟巻用に供出させられた。父は、半年で除隊になって帰ってきた。

極端な食糧不足のなか、写真館はまだ食えるだろうと縁者が集まってきて、一時は15人位の家族になっただろうか。もとより深瀬家に食糧などあろう筈もなかったが、父が来る者を決して拒まなかったというのは、自分が水呑み百姓の倅で、口減らしに奉公に出された痛みがあったからだろう。毎日、馬鈴薯と南瓜ばかり食べていた。そのせいか、いまだに南瓜だけは食べる気がしない。だが、御多分にもれず私も「生命惜しまぬ予科練の七つボタン」にあこがれる軍国少年だった。敗戦の昭和20年に妹可南子が生まれた。あの8月15日、近所の池野電器店のラジオで町の人たちと玉音放送を聞いたのだが、なんの感慨も残ってはいない。ただ、やけに暑

い日だったと思う。

　疎開児童も引揚げ、深瀬家の縁者たちも三々五々散っていった。私は5年生だった。

　中学は旧制の道立名寄中学、汽車通学だった。六・三・三制の発布された年で、私は旧制最後の生徒になったわけで、名寄中学が名寄高校に変わって2年生になるまで、4年間最下級生だった。

　高校2年生で下級生が入ってきたときは嬉しかった。まだ戦時の名残りで、上級生は威張って神様のような存在だった。わけもなく整列させられ、4年間毎日のようにビンタを張られていたので、「今にみていろ、下級生が入ってきたら今までの仇を討ってやる」と秘かに期待していたのだが、いざ下級生が入ってくる頃にはもうバンカラの気風も消えていて、いってみれば殴られ損だった。

　あいかわらずいつも腹がへっていたが、とても弁当など持っていける身分ではなく、昼食はいつもコッペパン一個だけだった。農家の伜だけは特権階級で、銀シャリのお辨当様を食べていた。深瀬家の食事も戦時中よりは昇格して、米三麦七くらいのごはんを食べられるようにはなっていたと思う。写真館の感材も乾板からフイルムに変わり、小型カメラもぼつぼつ出始めたが、まだ金はあっても物がない時代だった。

　初めてカメラを買ってもらったのは、高校1年生のときである。家の後継ぎの私に小型写真機も覚えさせた方がよかろうと思ってのことにちがいない。写真機といえば写場のアンソニーか組立暗箱しか使ったことのない私は、ボタンを押すとポンと蛇腹が飛出す「セミ・パール」はまさに魔法のビックリ箱のようなもので、しばらくは枕元において眠ったものである。当時使ったフイルムは「さくらパンF」のたしかＡＳＡ16だったと思うが、初めて写したのは学校の同じクラスのＳさんというあこがれの君だった。学校でカメラを持っているのは私一人、皆写されたがって私とカメラはとてももてたが、根が写真屋なのでしっかり実費だけはもらうことにしていたし、今から考えるとかなりの小遣いを稼いでいたように思う。

　深瀬写真館三代目となるべく、日大芸術学部写真学科に入学、津軽海峡を渡り、初めて東京に出てきたのは昭和27年、18才のときで、阿佐ヶ谷の屋根裏部屋に住んだ。戦後7年、まだ復興期の東京には闇市があり、そこここには瓦礫が残り、GIとパンパンガールが腕くんで歩き、食事は外食券食堂だった。その年血のメーデー事件があり、進駐軍は駐留軍となった。大学時代は一応の仕送りはあったもののとても足りず、アルバイトに追われていたが、夏休みと冬休みには栄養補給のため36時間列車を乗り継いで帰省した。

　卒業の年の春、ある女性と同棲することになって、郷里には帰るに帰れず、東京で広告会社に就職した。それが写真師と写真家の岐路になったと今しみじみ思う。

そして、生活に追われて郷里のことなど思い出す余裕もなく、弟が三代目を継ぎ10年以上が過ぎた。

三十代も半ばになって、どんなきっかけでかは忘れたが急に郷里が懐かしくなった。郷里といえば私にとって北海道の「深瀬写真館」であり血縁の人たちである。何度か足を運び、美深町の様子や父を中心とした家族を写した。名寄の妹夫婦も参加して宴会となりいつもにぎやかだった。2階の写場には昔使った八ツ切アンソニーが健在だった。皆で記念写真を写した。当時私はけれん味のある写真が好きで、ただの集合写真真では面白くないので、スパイスとして腰巻きヌードを配して一味つけようと企み（その頃私は腰巻きに凝っていた）、劇団員とか舞踏家とか知合いの女性に頼んでは美深町に連れて行ってモデルになってもらった。

父母の葬式用の写真も写した。妹に娘が生まれ、5才で亡くなった。写場での記念写真には途中10年近くのブランクがあるが、それは同じ配置で同じことをするのに飽きてしまったのと、北海道では他のテーマに集中していたせいである。昭和60年、礼文島でヌードを写す仕事があってひさしぶりにヌードを配して記念写真を写した。父はすっかり老いていて、もう永くはないなと思った。昭和62年正月、74才で死亡。お葬式に参列したあと父の遺影と家族の記念撮影をした。

あのアンソニーは今、美深町の洋品屋でショーウインドウのディスプレイに使われている。

写真、それは殯
トモ・コスガ

深瀬昌久は、戦後日本を代表する最も先進的かつ実験的な写真家の一人でありながらも作家活動の全貌が長らくベールに包まれていた数奇な人物である。1960年代から誌上を中心に、私性と遊戯に根ざした写真表現を発表し続け、1974年にニューヨーク近代美術館で開催された写真展「ニュー・ジャパニーズ・フォトグラフィー」において東松照明や川田喜久治、森山大道を含めた14名とともに出展作家として抜擢されたことをきっかけに国外でも認知され、写真集『鴉』(蒼穹舎、1986年)は今日における写真表現の傑作として世界的に高く評価されている。しかし1992年、行きつけのバーの階段から泥酔して転落。この時に受けた脳挫傷で重度の後遺症を負った深瀬は再び表舞台に姿を表すことなく、多くの謎を残したまま、2012年に78歳で永眠した。

　結果的に彼からカメラを奪うことになった事故の一年前、Inter Press Corporationより『家族』と『父の記憶』の二冊が写真集として刊行された。興味深いのは、そのどちらも彼自身の家族と故郷という極私的な題材を描いたものであったことだ。実に20年近い月日をかけて制作された大作と言っても良いこれらは、前者が伝統的な記念写真の形式に則って深瀬家の一族を定期的にスタジオ撮影したもので、後者が深瀬の父である助造を中心とした一族の日常をファミリーアルバムよろしく編んだものである。深瀬が追い求めた私性を象徴する最たる例とも言えるそれらがなぜ生み出されたのかについては、これまで語られる機会が限られてきた。そこで本稿では、深瀬が遺した発言を拠り所にしながら、謎めいた本作の背景に迫りたい。

1934年、深瀬は北海道北部に位置する美深町で祖父の代から写真館を営む一家に長男として生まれた。将来は三代目となって写真館を継ぐことを期待された彼は、幼少期から家業の手伝いを強いられた。中学に上がると丁稚奉公に出され、高校では写真部を創設。様々な写真雑誌の月例コンテストに応募する日々を送った。そして本格的な写真技術を学ぶために上京し、日本大学芸術学部写真学科に進学。このように写真館の跡取り息子として順当な道を歩んだが、事態はその後一転する。大学卒業後は当時の恋人と共同生活を送るために故郷には帰らず、

そのまま東京で生活することを選んだのである。それは写真館を継ぐ道を諦めることを意味し、家業の写真館は弟の了暉が継いだ。

　その後十数年間は、日進月歩で経済成長を遂げる東京での刺激的な生活に没頭するあまり故郷を顧みることもなかったが、三十代も半ばになって故郷と家族をふと懐かしんだ深瀬は、1971年の夏に当時の妻である洋子を伴って帰省する。弟の了暉と妹の可南子はそれぞれ結婚してどちらも既に子供に恵まれていたため、深瀬家はすっかり大所帯に成長していた。そこで深瀬は家族全員を写場（彼は写真館の撮影スタジオを"写場"と呼んだ）に集め、洋子だけを腰巻きひとつの半裸姿にさせて家族の中に投入して記念写真の撮影に挑んだ（図版2）のが、本作『家族』の始まりである。それと並行して、深瀬は助造を中心とした一家の日常を写真に記録し始め、これが後に『父の記憶』としてまとめられた。

　かつて「自分のテーマはいつも身近、手で触れられるものから始まる」[1]と言い残した深瀬はその言葉通り、それまでの東京での暮らしにおいては愛する女性達にレンズを向け続けたが、彼が抱えた無尽蔵の撮影欲求は最終的にいつも彼女達を傷つけた[2]。そのたびに深瀬も傷つき、「写真をうつしてるから写真家とはかぎらない、生きてるから生者でもない。ぼくはいったいなんだろう」[3]と実存的苦悩に苛まれた。そうした紆余曲折を経て辿り着いた故郷で彼が見つけた「身近」な被写体こそ、他でもない彼自身の肉親だったのだ。こうして始まった深瀬家を巡る撮影には、結果的に20年という長い歳月が費やされた。これほどの長期間にわたって彼がひとつの題材を突き詰めた作品というのは他に例がない。これが示すのは、深瀬の撮影欲求のルーツとも言える一家こそが彼のリビドーをまことに受け止めたという紛れもない事実である。

　本作の最も顕著な特徴は指摘するまでもなく、腰巻きを穿いた半裸姿の女性達の存在だ。腰巻きとは和服を着る際の肌着であり、既に洋服が大衆化した1970年代の日本においてはほぼ穿かれなくなったものである。撮影の初年には妻の洋子が腰巻きを穿いた半裸姿で登場し、その翌年には別の若い女性四名と深瀬の母みつゑが同様の格好でそれぞれ登場する。この腰巻きの対として、深瀬と助造が六尺褌を穿いて登場していることにも注目したい（図版17）。これも日本の伝統的な男性下着のひとつで、はるか昔に穿かれなくなったものだ。深瀬はこうした奇抜な衣装について「当時私はけれん味のある写真が好きで、ただの集合写真では面白くないので、スパイスとして腰巻きヌードを配して一味つけ」[4]たのだと説明する。さらに洋子以外の若い女性四名に至っては、深瀬が東京から連れてきた舞踏家や演劇学生であり、深瀬家とはなんら血縁関係にない。こうして出来上がった奇妙な写真を「深瀬写真館の三代目くずれである私の、パロディー」[5]と言い表している

ことから、「三代目くずれ」ならではの視点から家族写真に相応しくない要素（他人、裸、腰巻き、ふんどし、後ろ姿）を混入させることによって伝統的な家族写真の形式を皮肉ることが目的にあったと理解できる。

　1974年からの2年間は、半裸の女性達が登場しない代わりに深瀬自身が集合写真に写る（図版21）。それまで女性達が担ってきたポジションに立つと片手にレリーズケーブルを握り、シャッターは自ら切った。この年には紋付きの着物を着用した助造とみつゑの肖像写真（図版18,19）が撮られており、深瀬はそれらを「葬式用の写真」[6]と言い表している。すなわち遺影である。この年に撮られた助造の遺影は、後々の本作において重要な役割を果たすことになる。

　1975年の撮影を終えると本作は一旦中断された。その理由として深瀬は後に「同じ配置で同じことをするのに飽きてしまったのと、北海道では他のテーマに集中していたせいである」[7]と振り返るが、同年に助造が町で転倒し、それをきっかけに脚が不自由になっていることから、それまでのように気軽には記念撮影ができなくなったとも考えられる。以降、助造の老いは徐々に、しかし確実に進行していった。1984年、助造は美深町から100km離れた浜頓別町の特別養護老人ホームに入所した。

1985年5月、深瀬は雑誌の仕事でモデルや編集者らとともに礼文島へと向かっていた。その途中で美深町に立ち寄ったところ、助造がちょうど老人ホームから一時帰宅していたため、本作の撮影を10年ぶりに再開した。この時に伴ったモデルの女性には全裸で家族の中に混じらせ、撮影は弟子に任せて深瀬自身も被写体に加わった。「父はもう殆ど体がきかず、去年の暮れに特別養護老人ホームに入ったが、もう長くはあるまい。これが最後の記念写真かもしれない」[8]と深瀬が当時の心中を吐露したように、深瀬と助造が2人で写った写真では、かつての筋骨隆々とした助造の肉体は見る影もなくなり、すっかり痩せ細った姿が確認できる（図版29）。

　この年に撮られた家族写真には、他にも明らかな変化が見られる。深瀬の妹である可南子の娘、都の死である。本作の撮影が中断されていた間に幼くして亡くなっていた。その死を記録するために投入されたのが、写真の中で可南子が抱える遺影だ。奇妙なことに、生前の姿を捉えた遺影が逆説的にその死を提示する（図版26）。こうして仕上がった写真を眺めながら、深瀬は「ピントグラスに映った逆さまの一族のだれもが死ぬ。その姿を映し止める写真機は死の記録装置だ」[9]と言い残している。

　1987年1月、深瀬の父である助造は74歳で永眠した。葬儀の日、深瀬は喪服姿の一家を集め、いつものように記念撮影を始めた。それまで助造が立っていた場所には、ほぼ等身大の助造の遺影が置かれた（図版32）。「死の記録装置」によって

Fig.1: 深瀬昌久「Check! 4 あるばむ」(『アサヒカメラ』1973年9月号)

生み出された遺影は、同じ装置で再撮影されることによって、死が死を打ち消し、亡くなったはずの助造は写真の中でなお生き続けるようだ。まるで助造の死に気づかないかのように笑う一家の姿が、死の打ち消し現象を不気味に裏付ける。

　1989年になると登場人物が一気に減る。深瀬と母と弟、そして父の遺影が写るだけで、かつてのような賑やかさはない(図版33)。それもそのはずで、この年に深瀬写真館はとうとう廃業を迎えたのだ。写真館は弟の了暉が三代目を継いだが、時が経つに連れて過疎化が進む町での経営維持は難しく、最終的に廃業へと追い込まれた。かくして一家は四散となり、80年を超える深瀬家の歴史に終止符が打たれたのである。それは助造の死からわずか2年後のことだった。

　1991年、20年かけて撮影された家族写真は撮影年順にまとめられ、写真集『家族』が産声を上げた。もとは家族写真の軽快なパロディから始まった本作であったが、父の年老いた姿をきっかけに撮影は再開され、予想外の結末を迎えた。前半では家族の繁栄が、そして後半ではその衰退が示されることで、一家の栄枯盛衰が残酷なほど象徴的に記録されたのだ。つまり本作そのものが深瀬家の"遺影"であるとも言えるだろう。

自らの家族を遺影化するという構想は、実のところ深瀬によって、それこそ本作が撮り始められた当初から少しずつ練られていた節がある。

　1973年、深瀬は両親と弟とともに網走から知床半島までドライブに出かけた。このとき「今さらながら父も母も年老いた」[10]と感じた彼は、故郷で撮影した家族の写真(この一部は後に『父の記憶』に収録された)と1950年代に東京で撮影した写真

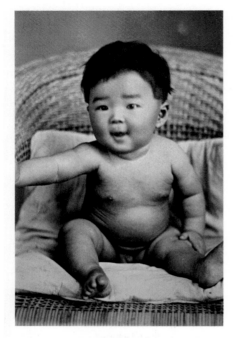

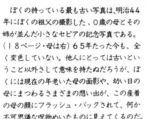

ぼくの持っている最も古い写真は、明治44年にぼくの祖父の撮影した、0歳の母とその姉が並んだ小さなセピアの記念写真である。(18ページ・母は右)65年たった今も、全く変色していない。他人にとっては古いということ以外さして意味を持たぬだろうが、ぼくには現在の年老いた母の面影や、幼い日の母にまつわるさまざまの想い出が、この産着の母の顔にフラッシュ・バックされて、何か不可思議な呪物めいたものに見えてくるのだ。

母が死んだら、多分この写真も一筋の煙となって消え去るにちがいない。

人は希望と失望と絶望と、すべての喜怒哀楽の象徴として、生涯一つの顔を持ちつづけるのだが、生から死への限られた時間の流れを、一瞬せき止める氷点として、不吉なるぼくらの写真術がある。

P11　ぼくと叔母
P12　五歳・祭りの日

P13　吉増剛造（詩人）
P14　三歳？
P15　坂本正治（エッセイスト）
P16　六歳 小学校入学式当日（オカッパ頭がぼく）
P17　都田豊三郎（牧師）
P18　0歳の母とその姉
P19　土方巽（舞踏家）
P20　母や叔父叔母たちと
P21　斉藤博亮（会社役員）
P22　左・二歳？右・深瀬洋子と猫のカボ

Fig.2: 深瀬昌久「顔」(『ロッコール』1976年1月号)

をそれぞれ上下に区分けしたフォトアルバム形式にまとめ、その冒頭には母と深瀬自身がそれぞれ生まれた年に深瀬写真館で撮影された記念写真を配置し(Fig.1)、「あるばむ」と題して誌上に発表。深瀬はそれを「否応なしに年月がたち、老人、若者、子供、私、いつか必ず死んでしまうこの世とやらは、私にとって、1冊の古びた『あるばむ』にはられた記念写真のようにも思えてきます」[11]と解説した。

　この時期に誌上発表された作品には、ページをアルバムに見立てた上で深瀬家の古いアルバムから引っ張り出してきた写真を起用したものが他にも幾つかある。「顔」と題された作品では、最後のページに深瀬が赤ん坊だった頃に撮られたスタジオ写真と掲載当時の妻の肖像写真を並べ、その下に「人は希望と失望と絶望と、すべての喜怒哀楽の象徴として、生涯1つの顔を持ちつづけるのだが、生から死への限られた時間の流れを、一瞬せき止める氷点として、不吉なるぼくらの写真術がある」[12]と書き加えた(Fig.2)。愛する人々は「いつか必ず死んでしまう」のだから、彼らが元気なうちに撮影することで「氷点」にせき止め、そうして仕上げた一家の遺影で「あるばむ」を作り上げるのだという意志が確かめられる。

　このような、いつの日にか訪れるであろう今生の別れを前もって予測することで彼の写真に滲み溢れる"先行した未練"というのは、本作『家族』においても同様に汲み取れるものだ。

結論として、本作で私達が見るものとは深瀬家の殯[13]である。生前の姿を鮮明に記録した遺影というものは、現代における殯の役割に近い。遺体が火葬された後も、仏間に飾られる遺影を目にすることで死者との思い出に浸ることができるからだ。深瀬が20年をかけて撮影してきたものは、単なる家族の記念写真ではなく、遺影とも言えるだろう。「ピントグラスに映った逆さまの一族のだれもが死ぬ」のだから、「死の記録装置」を使って「その姿を映し止め」ようとしたものだ。それは"先行した未練"がきっかけとなって、被写体となる人々が生命力溢れる頃から着手される。

　長い年月をかけて幾度となく写真という「氷点」にせき止められた家族の"遺影"の数々は、写真館の廃業をもって深瀬の眼前に並べられた。写真の中に凍結された家族は、その時々の生き生きとした姿を維持する。それらはまるで遺体が腐敗し、そしていずれは骨だけとなるような、徐々に家族が"朽ちていく"過程を段階的に示すかのようである。それらをあまねく凝視することは、まさしく殯の儀に等しい。少なくとも本作の編集段階においては、三代にわたって写真館を営んだ一家の歴史の喪に服す意味合いが込められていたに違いない。

　奇しくも『家族』刊行の翌年、深瀬は転落事故によって作家活動を閉ざし、その20年後に亡くなった。一家の"喪主"を務めた彼もまた故人となった今、深瀬家の"棺"とも言える本作は、本書の形となって再びこの世に紐解かれた。

　棺の中の彼らは目を開けたまま、じっと前方を凝視する。彼らと目が合った瞬間、深瀬家を巡る殯は、私達の中でにわかに、そして一方的に再開される。

1.　　田中長徳「深瀬昌久氏の場合 カラスを撮りに夏はインドへ」(『カメラ毎日』1982年8月号)
2.　　深瀬の伴侶として12年間を過ごした鰐部洋子は、彼と離別する3年前に「救いようのないエゴイスト」と題した原稿を発表。その中で深瀬との結婚生活について「10年もの間、彼は私とともに暮らしながら、私をレンズの中にのみ見つめ、彼の写した私は、まごうことない彼自身でしかなかった」(『カメラ毎日別冊 写真家100人 顔と作品』1973年)と振り返った
3.　　深瀬昌久「ドロまみれのザーメン」(『季刊写真映像』1969年9月25日号)
4.　　深瀬昌久『家族』跋文
5.　　深瀬昌久「ふるさと」(『アサヒカメラ』1972年11月号)
6.　　深瀬昌久『家族』跋文
7.　　同上
8.　　深瀬昌久「狂、礼文島。」(『流行写真』1985年8月号)
9.　　同上
10.　　深瀬昌久「Check! 4 あるばむ」撮影メモ(『アサヒカメラ』1973年9月号)
11.　　同上
12.　　深瀬昌久「顔」(『ロッコール』1976年1月号)
13.　　殯とは、古代日本で執り行われた葬送儀礼を指す。人が亡くなると棺に遺体を仮安置し、すぐには本葬を執り行わずに長期間を置いた。そうして遺体の腐敗や白骨化を目の当たりにする過程を経ることで、死を受け入れたとされている

Masahisa Fukase, 1991

In my earliest memories, I am always surrounded by people. My family, my neighbours, the three acacia trees that stood before our house, the huge elm tree growing by the entrance to my primary school, have all now become very precious to me – I treasure even the trees. I'm 57, and I suppose this deep attachment must be proof that I too am growing old, in the way that we all do.

'The current of the flowing river does not cease, and yet the water is not the same water as before. The foam that floats on stagnant pools, now vanishing, now forming, never stays the same for long. So, too, it is with the people and dwellings of the world.' [Kamo no Chōmei, *An Account of a Ten-Foot-Square Hut*, thirteenth century.]

My father died four years ago. And two years ago, my mother moved into a nursing home. My younger brother and his wife have divorced, and she lives in Tokyo with their two children. My sister and her husband, who retired from Japan National Railways when it was privatised, now live in Sapporo, where they manage a supermarket. The Fukase Photo Studio is now in the hands of someone else entirely. My family is scattered to the winds.

I was born in 2-21, Higashi-Ichijō, Bifuka, Nakagawa, on the northern tip of Hokkaido. My father's name was Sukezo, my mother's Mitsue. My grandfather Tsunemitsu came to Hokkaido originally from Yamagata Prefecture as a settler-farmer. During the Russo-Japanese War he joined the army, and was made a corporal. My grandmother Miyano, the daughter of a foot soldier in Edo times, was also apparently from Yamagata. It is not clear where my grandfather obtained his expertise in photography, but in 1908 he received a permit from local officials in Kamikawa to open a photography studio in Bifuka, where he also farmed a little on the side. My mother was their second daughter, born to them in 1911. My father was born in 1912, the third son of a farming family in Furen village, not far from Bifuka. As soon as he'd completed his compulsory education he was sent to work as a live-in apprentice in a photographic shop in the village. After nearly two years there, he moved to Sapporo to work for a small teashop supplying souvenir photographs to travellers. He became a 'touring photographer,' tasked with taking photographs at festivals and weddings in towns and villages, often travelling away from home for two weeks or a month at a time.

I clearly remember being made to do exactly this sort of thing by my father when I was a boy: he sent me out to work when I was still in junior high school. In the depths of winter, three days into January, he had me set up a booth with a sign saying 'Fukase Studio Sub-branch,' by a hotel near the station in the tiny village of Otoineppu, to wait for any customers that might come along. At village festivals I had to lay out rows of sample photographs next to booths selling cotton candy. I was so embarrassed – truth be told, I hated it.

There is no one alive now who might remember the details of how my father and my mother were introduced to one another, nor how it was decided he would be married into her family as an adopted son. They were married on an auspicious day in May of 1933: no doubt my grandfather took the commemorative photographs. By then my grandfather had had enough of being a photo-shop man, and he was happy to withdraw and let my father take over, as the second-generation owner of the shop. I was born in 1934. I was terrified of my father as a child. He had an extremely short temper, and he would fly into rages at the slightest thing. I was an amiable child, and intelligent, but in front of my father I was always timid and cowardly.

At that time, business in the photography trade was thriving. During New Year's, or at summer festivals, or on special occasions like the first day of school or graduation, long lines of people would form in front of the shop. Every one wanted a photograph to mark the occasion. In those days, owning a photography studio was a very prestigious thing.

It was my father's job to take the photographs, and to develop the plates (negatives didn't exist in those days; it was glass plates). He took great pride in his ability to prettify his shots, to straighten people's noses, firm up their mouths and level up their shoulders — there was no-one who could match him, he said. My mother's job was to print the photographs, and she did this using a contact printing machine, which we kept in a little dark room that was warmed by a charcoal brazier and always filled with the acrid smell of vinegar. The printing machine was about as high as I was, and I have a memory of standing by my mother as she timed the exposure of the plates, slowly muttering, 'One... Two... Three....' I think I must have been about three or four years old. I remember my mother often passed out from carbon monoxide poisoning. From the age of six, I was made to help her wash the prints. All the prints, of various sizes, 3 x 4.3 inches, or 4.5 x 6.5 inches, were put in a large vat, and I would rinse them with water, which I had to draw by pumping it from the well. When the water ran out, I would have to go and draw some more. Even in the depths of winter I had to do this, my hands numb with cold.

Soon after I had entered the local elementary school, the Great East Asia War began, and our school became a 'national elementary school'. In my second year at school, my younger brother Toshiteru was born. I remember the frenzied announcements from Imperial HQ about the victories of the Japanese Army, how we were going to exterminate each and every one of the 'British and America brutes'. But it was all bluster. Supplies were running out before our eyes, as was our food. And yet all they could tell us was 'Hold back your hunger till victory is won.'

Meanwhile, my father joined the Asahikawa infantry brigade of the Imperial Japanese Army. But after basic training he was sent out to provide help to farmers: going to work in the fields, wearing woollen army gaiters to scythe grass. By this time, we had nothing to sell in the shop, and we had to stop doing business, as did all the other shops. All the men in the village, with the exception of the young and the old, were being drafted and sent to fight. Anything made out of metal, whether it was bells from temples, iron braziers, tongs, anything at all, was being requisitioned for the war effort. Even my pet cat Tama was taken to provide the fur for the fur-lined collar of some soldier fighting in the north. After half a year in the army, my father was sent home.

Now there was a severe shortage of food, and relatives turned up at the house, apparently thinking that my family, with the business, would be able to provide for them. At one point, there were about fifteen of us living under one roof. Of course, we had no more food than anyone else, but my father never turned any-one away. Originally from a dirt-poor farming family, he had been sent away as a child because his family couldn't afford to feed him, so he knew how bitter it was to depend on others. Every day, all we ate was potatoes and pumpkins. Maybe it's because of that experience that to this day pumpkins are the one thing I can't bear the taste of. I of course was as fervently patriotic as the next boy: I wanted nothing more than to join the Yokaren cadets, the naval trainee pilots — to wear the 'seven brass-buttoned jacket' and 'willingly give my life', as the famous song went. In 1945, my sister Kanako was born. On August 15 1945, I listened along with the other people in the village to the Emperor making the 'Jewel Voice Broadcast', announcing Japan's unconditional surrender, in the Ikeno radio shop in my neighbourhood. I don't remember a single thing of what I felt at the time. The only thing I remember is that it was a searing hot day.

At war's end, the children who had been evacuated to the country left, and all the relatives who had been staying with my family went back to their homes. I was in the fifth grade of elementary school.

My junior high was Hokkaido Nayoro Junior High School, which I commuted to by train. The year after I entered junior high school, the school system officially changed to a new 6-3-3 plan [six years primary, three years junior high, and three years high school]. This meant that I was in the last year of the students who had entered junior high school under the old system, and there were no students in the years below me. This situation continued for four years, right up till my second year at high school, when Nayoro Junior High School became Nayoro High School.

When I reached the second year at high school, I was looking forward to having students in the years below me. One of the vestiges of war was that older students in school were treated like gods – they could do anything they wanted. For four years, older students had been making me stand to formal attention, and kept hitting me about the face, so I had secret plans to get my own back by doing the same to the younger boys. But by the time there were younger students, it was no longer acceptable to strut around playing the bullyboy. So – I really lost out: all that pain for nothing. I was still wandering around half-famished, but my family could not afford to send me to school with a home-packed bento lunchbox: a plain bread roll had to suffice. Only the children of farmers, who were the privileged class, ate bento lunches, with proper white polished rice. Even so, I remember as a family we were eating a lot better than we had during the war, though our mealtimes were certainly not lavish – our rice was still only three parts rice to seven parts barley. By now in the shop we were using negatives rather than plates, and the first portable cameras were beginning to appear. But there was very little in the shops, even if you had the money.

My father bought me my first camera when I was in my first year at high school, probably thinking that if I was going to take over the family business it was about time I got to know a little bit about photography. The only camera I had operated before that was the Anthony large-format view camera we had in the shop, so I was amazed at the way you could press a button on the Semi-Pearl compact folding camera, and the lens and shutter sprang forward on a bellows. To me, it was like a magic box, full of tricks and surprises. I was so pleased that for a time I slept with it by my pillow. The film was SAKURA PAN F film, ASA 16. I took my camera to school, and the first person I photographed was a Miss S, whom I had a crush on. I was the only person in the entire school who had a camera, and everyone wanted me to take their picture, so for a while I got a lot of attention from the girls. Naturally, as the son of a professional photographer, I made sure to be paid for my photographs. Now that I think about it, I must have made a fortune.

In 1952, at age 18, I left home and went to Tokyo, making the journey across the Tsugaru Strait between Hokkaido and Honshu, to study photography at Nihon University College of Art. This was to prepare me to take over the family business, as the third-generation heir. In my university days, I lived in a tiny attic room in a house in Asagaya. This was only seven years since the end of the war, and Tokyo was still getting back on its feet. There were black markets all over the place. Piles of rubble could still be seen in the streets, and GIs walked around with 'pan-pan girls' clinging to their arms. We would eat at wooden shacks and canteens. I was there during the Bloody May Day of 1952, and when the American occupation became the American troops 'stationed' in Japan. My father sent me a small allowance as a student, but it wasn't enough to live on, so I worked part-time jobs day and night. Every vacation, winter and summer, I would go back to Hokkaido, making the 36-hour trip back by train, so that I could feed myself up on my mother's nutritious food.

In the spring of my graduation year, I became involved with a certain woman, and we started living together. This made it quite impossible for me to go home, and I had to find employment with an ad agency in Tokyo. I now believe that this was a major turning point in my life, a fork in the road: I had to choose whether I wanted to be a *shashin-shi*, a 'studio' photographer, or a *shashin-ka*, an art photographer in the modern sense; I settled for the latter in the end. What with one thing and another, I then became completely preoccupied with my own daily life, with little time to think about what was happening back at home. My younger brother took over the business, and more than ten years passed.

And then, when I was in my late thirties — I can't quite remember why — I found myself missing my hometown. When I say hometown, I'm really talking about my family, and the Fukase Photographic Studio. I went back a number of times, and made photographs of scenes around Bifuka and of my father. My younger sister and her husband, who lived in Nayoro, would come over to the house, and food and drink would be brought out, with much boisterous merriment.

The Anthony camera we used in the old days was still up there on the first floor of the shop, still in fine fettle. We took a number of commemorative group photos. At the time, I had a rather pretentious streak, and I wasn't satisfied with ordinary, run-of-the-mill group lineups, so to add a bit of spice, and as an interesting variation, I had stage actresses and dancers from theatrical companies come and join us, and stand semi-nude, clad only in *koshimaki* in a few of the shots (I used *koshimaki* quite a bit in my photographs in those days). I took photographs of both my parents in preparation for their funerals. My younger sister had a baby girl, who died, aged five. After that, there was a period of ten years when I took no photographs at all in the family studio. This was partly because I had become bored with taking repeated family group portraits, but also because I was now preoccupied by another photographic theme when I made my trips to Hokkaido. And then, in 1985, I went to Rebun Island, to take some nude photos, and that spurred me to resume taking my family portraits: I now put one or two nudes in amongst family members. By then, my father was very frail, and I remember thinking to myself that he couldn't have long to go. He died in January 1987, at age 74. I took some commemorative photographs of all of us along with my father's funeral portrait.

That old Anthony camera of ours is now being used as a display item in the shop window of a Bifuka clothing store.

Archiving Death: The Family Portrait as a Site of Mourning
Tomo Kosuga

Masahisa Fukase (1934-2012) is considered one of the most radical and experimental photographers of the Japanese post-war generation. Yet for a long time the true breadth and originality of his art remained unknown. Fukase started attracting attention for his photographs in the 1960s, mainly in photographic journals, where they were noted for their highly personal nature and playfulness. In 1974, pieces by Fukase were included in a ground-breaking exhibition at New York's Modern Museum of Art titled 'New Japanese Photography', which featured work by 15 photographers, including Shomei Tomatsu, Kikuji Kawada, and Daido Moriyama. 1986 saw the publication by Sokyusha of Fukase's collection *Karase* (*Ravens,* 1975-1986): it was widely hailed as a photographic masterpiece. However, in 1992 Fukase suffered a traumatic brain injury after a fall down the steep stairs of his favourite bar in Tokyo. It left him utterly incapacitated until his death in 2012. It is only recently that the wealth of material left by this legendary photographer has started being disclosed.

In 1991, the year before Fukase suffered his accident, which essentially marked the end of his creative life, the Inter Press Corporation published two collections of his photographs, titled *Kazoku* (*Family*) and *Chichi no Kioku* (*Memories of Father*). Both these collections were intensely autobiographical, dealing with his family and his hometown in Hokkaido. In fact the photographs in these major works were taken over a considerable length of time, almost two decades. *Family* comprised photographs taken of Fukase's larger family (including the spouses and children of his younger brother and younger sister) in the family's photographic studio, and ostensibly it is a collection of family photographs. The latter takes the guise of a family photograph album, with pictures of scenes in the Fukase family's ordinary daily life, with a focus on Masahisa's father Sukezo. At first sight, they may seem like quintessential examples of the kind of highly personal work Fukase had always pursued. However, it seems to me that they have a particular, extra significance. In this essay, I want to delve into the background of the enigmatic work *Family*, and to examine how it differs from his other work, with evidence provided by Fukase's own comments and observations.

Fukase was born in 1934, in a small town called Bifuka in northern Hokkaido. He was the eldest son of a successful studio photographer. By the time he was born, the business had been in the family for two generations, and it was an unspoken assumption that when he grew up he would take it over, as the third-generation owner. As a young boy, he helped his parents in the shop, and was also sent out to work in a travelling capacity, to neighbouring towns and villages, at festivals and other occasions. At high school, he set up a photography club: he subscribed to various magazines, submitting entries to photographic competitions, and avidly perusing their columns to see if his work got a mention. After graduating from high school, Fukase went to Tokyo, entering the Photography Department of Nihon University College of Art to get a thorough grounding in photography. Thus far he had followed the expected path of a model son. However, this was not to last. On graduation from university, rather than go home he chose to stay on in Tokyo, to live with the woman with whom he was involved at the time. In effect, this meant he had to abandon the expectations of his family, and his brother Toshiteru took over the family business in his place.

For the next ten years Fukase threw himself into the excitement of life in Tokyo, which was fast becoming a modern metropolis, with no thought at all for what was going on back at home in Hokkaido. But then, in his late thirties, he got a sudden yearning to see his family and hometown. In the summer of 1971 he took a trip home, accompanied by Yoko, his second wife. His younger brother Toshiteru, and his younger sister Kanako, had married, and had children of their own, so the Fukase family had considerably expanded, encompassing several generations. It was partly to celebrate this that Fukase had all the members of the family gather together in the 'shooting place' (shajō; this was what Fukase called the studio). A photograph he took on this occasion, of the whole family arranged with Yoko semi-naked, clad only in a thin cotton koshimaki, or waist-wrap [Plate 2], became the first work in what eventually, two decades later, was published as the present collection Family. At the same time, Fukase started recording scenes from his family's daily life, with a focus on his father, and these photographs he later put together as Memories of Father.

Fukase's subject matter in Tokyo had always centred on his domestic life, in particular the women with whom he was involved, whom he photographed continually, to the point of obsession. 'My material always starts with what is nearest, with the people I can just reach out and touch,' he wrote.[1] In the end, however, Fukase's relentless obsession with photographing the women in his life proved too much for them, and it contributed to their decision to leave him.[2] After each relationship breakdown, Fukase was devastated, and he went through bouts of existential despair. 'Taking photographs does not make you a photographer, and living doesn't make you alive. At the end of the day, who am I really?' he wrote.[3] And in 1971, after a long series of emotional twists and turns, and once again back in Hokkaido, it was the people who were closest to him, his own family, whom he turned to for the material for his photographs. As things turned out, he would end up spending an extraordinarily long time, more than twenty years, on this project. On no other topic did he expend so many years, nor concentrate so devotedly. If there is one thing this demonstrates, it is surely that his family, who lie at the root of his obsessive need to capture and hold people on camera, recognized his artistic impulse, and valued it.

The most noticeable feature of the present collection is of course the presence of several semi-naked women, who we see in koshimaki, light cotton waist wraps. These light waist wraps were what women traditionally wore next to their skin under kimonos. By the 1970s, however, everyone had adopted western clothing: hardly anyone wore koshimaki any more. In the first year that photographs were taken for this collection, Fukase's wife Yoko is dressed in a koshimaki. The following year, in a number of photographs, four other women appear similarly clad, as does Fukase's mother Mitsue. In one photograph [Plate 17], Fukase and his father wear the traditional male fundoshi, the cotton loincloth, while the women are in koshimaki. The loincloths, a form of traditional underpants for men, also belonged to another age. As for why he got his subjects to dress so bizarrely, Fukase writes in his Afterword, 'At the time, I had a rather pretentious streak, and I wasn't satisfied with ordinary, run-of-the mill group line-ups, so to add a spice, and as a bit of interesting variation, I had stage actresses and dancers from theatrical groups come and join us, and stand semi-nude, clad only in koshimaki in a few of the shots.'[4] Apart from Yoko, the young women wearing koshimaki were more or less strangers. Elsewhere, Fukase wrote that these photographs were a 'parody', taken by 'myself, the third-generation son, the loser' [sandaime kuzure de aru watakushi no parodeii].[5] It would seem that the purpose of incorporating such incongruous elements (non-family-members, nakedness, koshimaki, fundoshi, subjects who turn their backs to the camera) was to poke fun at the traditional idea of the family photograph from the perspective of some-one who felt himself a family failure.

For two years after 1974, the photographs include no women from outside the family: instead Fukase himself makes an appearance [Plate 21]. Now, where previously the women stood, he stands, holding the shutter release cable. In the same year, 1974, Fukase had his mother and father dress in traditional formal attire, black kimonos with the family crest, so that he could take photographic portraits of each of them [Plate 18, 19]. These were no ordinary portraits, however, but rather, as he explains in his Afterword, specifically for use in their funerals - they were *i-ei,* or photographic memorial portraits, taken of the living to be used after their death.[6] The photograph he took of the yet-to-be deceased Sukezo would, after Sukezo's death, play an important role in later photographs.

The photographs Fukase made in 1975 marked the end of a phase, and for a while he took a rest from this project. The reason, Fukase was later to claim, was 'firstly that I had become bored with taking repeated family group portraits, and secondly, because I was now preoccupied by another photographic theme when I made my trips to Hokkaido'.[7] A third reason may have been that in 1975 Fukase's father Sukezo had a fall, which left him debilitated, so that it was now a much more difficult proposition for him to join everyone else for a commemorative photograph. After this fall, Sukezo's age started to tell on him, slowly but discernibly. In 1984, he was moved to a special nursing home for the elderly, in a small town called Hamatonbetsu, located 100km from Bifuka.

In May 1985 Fukase took a trip to Rebun Island, off the northern tip of Hokkaido, accompanied by a model and an editor, on a photographic shoot. On the way, they stopped off in Bifuka, and it so happened that Sukezo was at home on a visit from his nursing home. It was at this point that Fukase resumed taking photographs for the series, after an extended break of 10 years. Fukase now had the models who were accompanying him appear completely naked in some of the photographs, and he included himself in the line-up, getting his assistant to press the shutter release. 'My father has become very feeble indeed, and toward the end of last year he entered a home for the elderly,' he wrote. 'I can't think he has long to go. These could well be the last photos I take of him.'[8] In the photograph of Fukase and his father, just the two of them, Sukezo's old age is stark: his once robust, muscular frame is nowhere to be seen, and he is emaciated and frail [Plate 29].

There is another event in the life of the family that is evident from the photographs taken on this occasion. Fukase's younger sister Kanako had a daughter, Miyako, who had died during the decade in which Fukase had stopped taking photographs of the family. In order to record the death of this child, Fukase chose to incorporate in his photograph another *i-ei,* or photographic memorial portrait, of Miyako, which Kanako holds behind her. In a strange way, the photograph of the deceased, which captures the child as she was when alive, paradoxically provides the viewer with a notification of her death [Plate 26]. 'My entire family, whose image I see inverted in the frosted glass, will die one day,' Fukase once observed. 'This camera, which reflects and freezes their images, is actually a device for archiving death.'[9]

In January 1987, Fukase's father Sukezo breathed his last. He was 74 years old. On the day of the funeral, Fukase gathered the whole family together dressed in formal mourning attire, and took the usual commemorative group portrait. The spot where Sukezo had previously stood was now occupied by a nearly life-size photographic memorial portrait, the very same portrait Fukase had taken in preparation several years before [Plate 32]. The re-appearance of the funeral portrait - produced using a device that archives death - in a photograph generated by the same device, suggests Fukase is arranging for death to cancel out death. Sukezo, who is supposed to be deceased, is still there. The way the family all look, laughing and smiling merrily, as if completely unaware that he has died, seems eerily to emphasize this impression.

By 1989, there is a noticeable reduction in the size of the family. It now consists merely of Fukase, his mother and his brother, who pose with the commemorative portrait of his deceased father. There is not a trace of the merriment we saw earlier [Plate 33]. This was only to be expected: the Fukase Photographic Studio was about to be closed down. Fukase's younger brother Toshiteru had carried on the family photographic studio in his elder brother's place, but as time passed, with increasing migration to the cities, the population in the town had shrunk and the business had come to a standstill. The family were about to disperse to various parts of the country, marking an end to the eighty-year era in the history of the family. This all happened within two years of Sukezo's death.

Fig. 1: Fukase Masahisa, 'Check! 4 Album', *Asahi Camera*, September 1973.

Such were the circumstances in which Fukase put together the photographs he had taken over so many years and published them as this book, simply titled *Family*.

A series that started out as an amusing parody of conventional family photographs changed halfway through and by the time the work was resumed, with the enfeeblement and death of Fukase's father and the untimely death of his niece, took on an increasingly sombre tone. The first half of the book shows a family that is thriving; the second, shows the family in marked decline. In effect what it ends up recording, painfully and symbolically, is the story of one family's rise and subsequent fall. In a sense the collection itself ends up being a kind of *i-ei*, or photographic memorial portrait, that tells of the demise of the photographer's family.

Interestingly, a careful reading of Fukase's writings shows that the idea of creating a series of portraits of his family to pre-emptively memorialise it, may very well have been part of his intention from the start.

In 1973, Fukase had set out with both parents and his brother for a drive along the coastal route from Abashiri to the Shiretoko Peninsula. Fukase noted how much his mother and father seemed to have aged – though of course he had been aware of it for some time.[10] At this point, Fukase was putting together a collection that seems like an 'album' of photographs of his family in Bifuka (some of which would be published later in *Memories of Father*), with photographs of his life in the 1950s in Tokyo, which he juxtaposed at the top and bottom of each page. Published under the title *Album*, the series begins with two photographs, taken in the Fukase Photographic Studio, the first of himself as a baby, the second of his mother as a baby, each with dates [Fig. 1]. Fukase wrote: 'In this world time passes inexorably, and everyone will die. It seems to me now that all of us – old, young, children, even I myself - are like nothing so much as photographs stuck inside a very old photograph album.'[11]

Other collections published in photography journals at this time feature photographs that Fukase seems to have just taken straight out of family albums. In a collection titled 'Face', the final page has a baby photo of Fukase himself positioned alongside a portrait of Yoko from a series he was publishing at the time [Fig. 2]. Underneath it Fukase records his thoughts: 'Each of us has but a single face, which in the all too short span of a human life serves as the symbol of hope, disappointment, despair, the whole variety of human emotions we all experience. The black art of people such as myself, who are photographers, allows us to freeze the allotted life that flows from the birth to the grave that

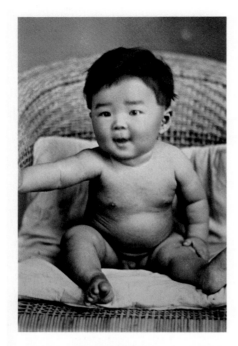

ぼくの持っている最も古い写真は、明治44年にぼくの祖父の撮影した、0歳の母とその姉が並んだ小さなセピアの記念写真である。（18ページ・母は右）65年たった今も、全く変色していない。他人にとっては古いということ以外さして意味を持たぬだろうが、ぼくには現在の年老いた母の面影や、幼い日の母にまつわるさまざまの想い出が、この産着の母の顔にフラッシュ・バックされて、何か不可思議な呪物めいたものに見えてくるのだ。

母が死んだら、多分この写真も一筋の煙となって消え去るにちがいない。
　人は希望と失望と絶望と、すべての喜怒哀楽の象徴として、生涯一つの顔を持ちつづけるのだが、生から死への限られた時間の流れを、一瞬せき止める氷点として、不吉なるぼくらの写真術がある。

P11　ぼくと叔母
P12　五歳・祭りの日

P13　吉増剛造（詩人）
P14　三歳？
P15　坂本正治（エッセイスト）
P16　六歳,小学校入学式当日(オカッパ頭がぼく)
P17　都田豊三郎（牧師）
P18　0歳の母とその姉
P19　土方巽（舞踏家）
P20　母や叔父叔母たちと
P21　斉藤博亮（会社役員）
P22　左・二歳？右・深瀬洋子と猫のカボ

Fig. 2: Fukase Masahisa, 'Face', *ROKKOR*, January 1976.

this single face symbolises in one brief moment of time.'[12] Conscious that all the people who are dear to him 'will die one day', as a photographer the only thing he can do is to 'freeze their images' for a brief moment, memorializing them, and then create an album of such memorializing portraits. It is this strong pre-emptive attachment to the people in his life who he knows will one day depart that we sense overflowing in Fukase in the present collection *Family*.

I would suggest that when we look at this collection we are participating in a form of mourning. . In ancient times in Japan, in a practice referred to as *mogari*, the body of the deceased would lie 'in state' for a while, as the mourners gathered around praying, beseeching the dead person to return, and even tempting them to do so with rites and festivities. Eventually, the changes that occurred in the body would allow the bereaved to recognize and accept that their loved one had died. The photographic portraits known as *i-ei* commemorating the deceased person (taken while they were still living) that today figure in Japanese funeral rites play a role that is very similar.[13] Even after the body has been cremated, and the ashes put into the Buddhist altar, the mourners are able, by looking at the memorial photographs, to immerse themselves in the memory of the deceased. The photographs Fukase took of his family were no ordinary family photographs, but rather memorial photographs, to be used after their subjects' death. Since, as he wrote, everyone he caught on his camera, his entire family, was going to die, the only thing he could do in the face of that inevitability was to use the camera, that 'device for archiving death,' to freeze their image in time. This was something he had to do pre-emptively, when the person who would die was still brimming with life. With the death of his father, which symbolised the demise of the whole family, after two decades of freeze-framing his family, these photographs of the now deceased persons could be laid out for him to view. As we look at the collection, we see each and every member as they were at particular moments in their life. However, there is no bringing them back: they are gone for good. As we turn the pages, we witness the gradual decay of the family setting in, shown stage by stage, in a way that brings to mind the way that a dead body gradually decomposes, leaving nothing but bleached bones. By looking head-on at these 'caskets' that hold his loved ones, Fukase attempts to mourn their departure, to comfort the spirits of the dead, and to come to terms with his loss.

Tragically, the year after *Family* was published, Fukase had his fall, which meant the end of his life as a photographer. Twenty years later, he died. Today, the chief mourner of the family is no longer alive, but this book, to which he has consigned the dead body of his family, remains with us. We gaze at the members of this family, and they all stare back at us. As we meet their staring eyes, we may feel that the process of the mourning vigil, conducted around the Fukase family, is taking place within ourselves.

1. Tanaka Chotoku, 'Fukase Masahisa: To India, for shots of crows in summer'. *Camera Mainichi*, August 1982.
2. In 1973 Fukase's second wife Yoko Wanibe published an article in the *Camera Mainichi* supplement titled 'The Incurable Egoist'. 'In the ten or so years or our marriage, he has only seen me through the lens of a camera, never without. And in fact what he saw through the lens was not me, but nothing other than himself.'
3. Fukase Masahisa, 'Infortune/Pitiful Sperm', *The Photo Image*, 25 September 1969.
4. Fukase Masahisa, Afterword, *Family*.
5. Fukase Masahisa, 'Hometown'. *Asahi Camera*, November 1972.
6. Fukase Masahisa, Afterword, *Family*. Fukase states that the photographs were taken 'in preparation' for their funerals.
7. Ibid.
8. 'Perfumed Colors 8 – Madness, Rebun Island', *Ryūkō Shashin*, August 1985.
9. Ibid.
10. Fukase Masahisa, 'Check! 4 Album', memo, *Asahi Camera*, September 1973.
11. Ibid.
12. Fukase Masahisa, 'Face', *ROKKOR*, January 1976.
13. Mogari refers to a funeral ritual that would take place in ancient Japan. The body of the deceased would lie in its coffin, without being given a proper funeral, for a considerable amount of time, allowing the bereaved to recognize and accept that their loved one had died.

MASAHISA FUKASE
FAMILY

Published by MACK
Originally published in 1991 by Inter Press Corporation of Japan

© 2019 Masahisa Fukase Archives for the images
© 2019 Masahisa Fukase and Tomo Kosuga for their texts
© 2019 MACK for this edition

With thanks to Takuya Fukase, Yoko Miyoshi, Kanako Daikoji, Hisashi Daikoji, Akiko Akai, Kyoko Fukase, Gaku Daikoji, Saga Kobayashi, Atsushi Hamanaka, Michael Hoppen, Russet Lederman and Jeff Gutterman.

Design by Morgan Crowcroft-Brown
Translation by Lucy North
Printed in Italy

978-1-912339-57-0
mackbooks.co.uk